MID-RIVER

MID-RIVER

DALE ZIEROTH

Anansi   Toronto

Some of the poems here have been published in or accepted for:
Queen's Quarterly, NeWest ReView, West Coast Review,
CBC *Anthology, Waves, Raven, Grain* and *Canadian Literature.*

The author and publisher are grateful for the support of
the Canada Council and the Ontario Arts Council.

Photograph: Marge Zieroth
Cover design: Joss Maclennan
Typeset and printed by The Coach House Press, Toronto

House of Anansi Press Limited
35 Britain Street
Toronto, Canada M5A 1R7

Canadian Cataloguing in Publication Data

Zieroth, Dale.
Mid-river

(House of Anansi poetry; HAP 39)
Poems.

ISBN 0-88784-084-1 pa.

1. Title.

PS8599.I37M52   C811'.54   C80-094771-1
PR9199.3.Z53M52

Contents

For Marge and Laura
and for friends in the blue valley
with special thanks to Dennis and Ian

The Columbia Valley lies between the Purcell and Rocky Mountains of British Columbia. Invermere is situated there, on Lake Windermere. Cranbrook is to the south, Golden to the north. Calgary is a four-hour drive to the east, over the Continental Divide and through Kootenay and Banff National Parks.

Baptism

In mid-river we join the ancient force
of mud and leaves moving in their journey
down the face of the continent and after
the first dance of leaving
one element for another, we fall quiet,
waiting for the silence to give us a
glimpse of history. In mid-river, it is
still possible to imagine Thompson's world,
without roads or bridges, rivers that
go back beyond white lives into the rocks
that push and fold, fault and break
as the new world rises from
the old.
        Yet this is still our river.
It does not matter that we are not
the first, what we will find today
has been found a hundred times before: it is
the ancient story of men meeting water,
as if there were a time, or faith,
when all of us were rivers, one
strength sliding out of the sky and into
the sea, one direction in us all.

But the river churns here and beats along the shore.
It picks up speed on the outside curve
cutting past the cottonwoods and under the deadfalls
that sweep across the water like the last arm of the land
and the water takes command.
I bend my paddle in my hand and my friend
digs in but there are branches like dead fingers in our faces
and there can be
no avoidance now, water comes up up and the
snag bends us down until my lungs
are in the water they are stones and I am
grabbing for the tree as if it were
my friend while the current sucks on me and my arms

go heavy as lead, a scream
goes dead in my throat, we do not
belong here, it bubbles and swallows
silt, the taste of ice,
there are blue stars somewhere and all the sounds of water
are alive and they pour in my ears,
into my eyes as if the river is already sure
how deep it will carry me,
what it will do with my skin, how it will dissolve
and burst and thin out the blood and I roll over
in a dream of clouds, willows, catch the edge
of a bank beaver's hole, brown mud like gold on my palm,
my feet still pulling for the ocean and then they find
gravel, the river rock, the river
pushes me away and I am shaking in the air again,
shaking for my friend riding the canoe's bottom
like a drunken pea pod, he grinds on the bank
a hundred yards downstream, his boots sucked off,
his body like a hole in the sand.

I breathe in the sun, take it yellow
into the body that spits grey in the river.
The baptism is over.
We have walked away without the grace of
fish or grebes, and the river is still the same.
I sit and watch the water with the oldest eyes of men:
if I trust the river, I will be
caught in it, rolled backwards into the
simplest race of all, the first, and the river is hard, it is
carnal and twists like an animal going blind in the rain,
but it leaves me pouring water from my shoe and then I see
him stand, wave, we have
first words.
Soon our paddles will bite the water but they will not
break it: our place on earth is rich enough,
the sudden rush of birdsong, our own
mid-river laughter as the warmth begins again.

Floe Lake

for Ian

1.

We climbed through summer towards the lake
as if the lake were all
the promises we needed, climbing hard
through the larkspur and the
elderberry, friends ahead and friends
behind, the world in order
coming with us to the lake.

At the switchbacks we met
the first of the strange new flowers coming
through the snow as if this were
the very beginning of life.
Under each tree, where the snow had gone,
we watched the spreading circle of spring
and looked into the meadows and into
the trees where each man heard inside himself
words he had never heard
before. Until the lake
which put an end to words.

2.

The mountain stands up
on the broken feet of its glacier,
tosses rock, then ice down into the lake where the water
moves like the breaking of mirrors,
or birds jumping into flight, ptarmigans
catching on the edge of the glacial wind
that sucks me out of the scrawny trees, the broken
dwarfs of treeline

and only the lake is
approachable, at the shore where the harmonicas
and fires are already warming up,
the noises of tent and pack as the mountain booms again,
fills the camp with
silence as white and endless as the
cornice that dives for the lake

this is the place to sleep
where the lake hugs the Rock Wall and is
content to be small and green and ice
nine months of the year, our dreams will
scale the face of the mountain all night long
this is how we will connect and disappear
not falling but
flying, hooked together in
hand to hand combat with the rocks up above
the ice floes that sail like swans
across the lake and past the dreamers who are
stirring in the yellow dawn, tasting the stars in their coffee

3.

Coming back, we begin by forgetting,
where we are going now there is no room
for perfection. Once there was
a bird to remember, the way it flew, the call
it made, another time
the colour of a tree. Or the young men
standing all along the shore
feeling as strong and as wild in their minds as
the water itself. These things
are making room for the highway that is
a dark line on the mountain.
We are half-way back and the loss
comes down like rain. I have found
another place to leave behind like a home
and only these friends will bind me to it, this
smell of rock on their hands, these men
in the same rain all around me
like the shy sound of wind across water. ? simile

Strong social collective sense
in this preceding poems!

Tourism: Words from a Park Employee

1.

I have the blue earth here,
over here, could you gather over here for a moment,
I have a holy place here
I can heal you
I can show you where the young men grow still at last
We can drink the wonder and there will still be
left-overs high as silver peaks
this way, step
around your weariness, just for a moment
let the perfect world be seen

2.

The car's turned up like a turtle
on the side of the road, on the grass where
Okanagan apples roll from the busted trunk

and two people stand very still
dark stains on their clothes, their hands up near
their faces
their grey private faces
and they stand close to the car and look down

This is how they come
looking for the perfect picture at
60 m.p.h.

and only a handful
learn to slow down, maybe the Californians can
not the farmers from
Iowa or Saskatchewan
and the big tubs of

Winnebagos can never stand the pace
they wallow till noon in their campgrounds
and start out late and hunt through till dark and

can't find the comfort or the beauty or anything

                                   safe
                                 that's what

               they're after
               no bears
               no Hell's Angels either

               so I speak to them
               and they go away to their chesterfield
               dreams

      3.

I speak to them in campgrounds, out of pamphlets,
I whisper into their ears as they
turn another corner into rock and
the wild animals half-tame now,
the alpine glowing in the evening light,
I am there,

Redstreak Campground, 200 watch me
pushing pictures through the machine,
making up excuses on the screen,
pin-pointing places they'd rather be,
and the adolescent girls at the back
are noisy and alive like the young
everywhere and I
yell at them over the microphone: thus we
contact one another and it's a joke here
and now time for a frown and so I try

  answering their questions without
  a laugh
        for these are people like myself
  they would like to find out

  who I am
  in the time it takes on TV
  and I think of them as captive, like those
  pictures still in my head:

  someone down on the ground like an animal
  hazard lights flashing at the moon

a man running, a kid in pain
a woman sick on the yellow line

Good evening and
look at this: road-kills and
elk heads and skinned out bears as red as a dead man
look at what the garbage has done
look at the moose and the marten flattened out
look at the earth
look at the rotten policies ✳

this is supposed to be a good place
where can you go anymore

    4.
And I try
and I want to tell them everything I
have, each sizzle and we do
                sometimes share
                one world
  but they are on holiday from life
  so thank you and good night

and one by one, they leave:
the women holding their children and their men,
the club jackets and the baseball caps,
cans of insect repellent in one hand
pamphlets falling from another

and there isn't anything I can say
that they'll remember
after they've driven another six hundred miles
the next day

the last one drifts by
smiling
talks a bit: he's from Calgary, knows

  about bears
  and thanks he says,

  did you take all those pictures yourself

Birth

They said the first six weeks
would be the hardest   they said there would be
resentment and then the guilt
my wife would not love the child instantly
and both of us would run
I would be hemmed in like a
fighter going down for the last time
I would long for
a single night's sleep
the undisturbed dawn   a day away from
the stink of things   that much time
without the guilt
knowing exactly how long
I'd been away from home   how much
she needed me   my wife and the child thing
that bound me to her like pain   bound me
to so much of the world that could only mean
money and time   work and eat
They said it would happen that way
I would become an adult   birth
was part of that job
They smiled when they asked their questions
and those who had children of their own
they could wait   they could
wonder when I would finally
catch fire   would it take a year or maybe
ten?   And I remember too
what they said   it gets better

Better when the child
begins her own story   a smile
to start with   looking back at somewhere
inside your head and that's the signal
everything is going to be
all right   The day she learned there were rules in the world
she learned to duck coming out from under tables
making noises that sound like questions

filling in a space around us
we didn't know was there
After her bottle and her blanket   after
her mother there is me
big old man no longer afraid to tell a stranger
the tiny words of love   love and the need
to be charged again by something human
like the morning when her arms go up to me
Will she speak today   will the word
burn and glow   catch fire in my mind
empty it till there is nothing
but the sound of blood speaking to blood

She stands by the window
almost a year   It took me
twenty-nine years to reach this place beside her
They said this would be
such another place   I did not know
there were babies everywhere and mothers who can
hold us all together   There is something
familiar in me again that
makes me big   Now it is my turn to say
I understand   I have been inside that room
with the lights and the doctor when
she shimmers in the air like viscera
I hear her lungs explode as the blood
turns in its place and is home   look god look she is
alive like her father who stands up inside his eyes and is
delivered to the good world again

Flying the Valley

Up in the high cold where everything
turns cold, turns blue, it all comes clear,
the pattern of snowmobile tracks circles the trees like wolves
while the valley spreads and leaps and
spreads again one more time
up above the smoke from sawmills and then is lost
beyond the last dark raven that hurls itself
like a black mark on the wind
back into the dirt. The little things below get
swallowed up in the curvature of earth, gone at last
the flat of the valley, lost
and little valley.
The most important things happened here
200 years ago. David Thompson came through
wrote a page in his journal
and was gone.
Up in the air it all comes clear
it was time to get out of there
Valley View, Valley Auto, Valley Florists, Valley Foods
and it makes me laugh
now that I can see it from
this high.

Below me is the usual tourist town:
on the 24th of May the takeover is complete, the act
is performed openly in the streets.
In the winter, the town returns
to its own blood again: occasionally there is
an unwed mother,
the mix and match of wives until there are
scenes in the Legion and then some fights
with just the right amount of blood, the usual things
go on: a suicide in April, another in the fall,
a fat lady
a beach
ask anyone who has heard their fathers talking
ask how much their town has changed   as if they think
they are exempt from the world

and sometimes they worry when the
taxes come and the governments come and go like
promises   it is that kind of town, it
makes the hippies laugh
which makes the merchants mad: at least *they* look ahead.
Each fall, before the ground is hard
they dig a dozen graves.

We go through Sinclair Pass
where the Indians once came
dragging their famous Europeans behind.
We go around and feel the sun turning in its
socket and we dip and bank and climb
until we are ready to go
home again. We see the cars at last, we know who is down there,
the men in their groups talking about
the world inside their weather and some of them
will die that way. The rest will talk about
the old families of Cleland and Kirsch
Tegart and Coy. And some of us will want
pioneers coming out again from England
coming down the river in a boat full of animals,
some of us would like those dreams
another chance to
plan and survive and plan again,
building ourselves up but always remembering
the blue mountains that come running down at us
from all the corners of the earth   the way
they let us know how much
has already been done,
finding time to plant and grow
knowing neighbours   slowing down   gathered together
as perfect as the scenery but now we are
circling one last time
getting ready to touch down and the mountains
jump back to their places while I
roll on and on through a lifetime of
valleys and peaks, dreams, flatness, cold and haze,
until the dirt slows me down in the end.

Against the World

for Marge

When I come against the world
and fall apart,
when the notion of disaster comes,
my own, yours, all of us operating the collective planetary
error that sends us wheeling out of orbit and into the
wanton dark, when I am gutted and
hung like a hundred others in a nameless iron place,
when I ache from failure
and my plans are dead and stacked around me
like stones, then I know
you will never love me now.
I throw my anger like a cloak
over you.
       Yet if my last move is weak, it still
moves to include you.

Fight then, fight if you have to.
Chop into our bond with the
bright axe of your anger. Bring out
the litany of threat and regret until they jump like
spark and fuel, but let us also
see clearly how love can finally
carve and quip inside the duel and dance at last
out through the two of us,
watch for the moment when love
throws a shadow on all the shapes of the world
and for a while has the key that can keep it
carefully locked away, when we
heal and agree to wrap around
each other like a rag around
a wound, around the dread that comes through me,
then we can
come against the world together, sometimes smiling
sometimes stopping dead when we see
how much of our faces have already been
worn and washed away, smoothed
and drained into the common public street
where we live.

Coyote Pup Meets the Crazy People
In Kootenay National Park

Brian brought him in
dumped in the back of his warden's truck and we watched him
die, a gasp at a time
spaced so far apart we knew he was
gone but suggested this or that anyway,
his breath hooked on a bone in his lungs,
his brown sides heaving for the sky
and we all felt for him in our different ways
which are the differences between men.
And twice Larry said, 'Poor little fellow.'
And Brian: 'I could give him a shot of 'nectine
or a bullet but all I've got
is the .270 and that's
too big.' So we hung on
till Ian pushed down on his ribs:
'Not much there.' And still we
wanted him to run like the wind for the bush.
'Is that it?' I asked, hearing his
last lunge at the air, which it was, anyone
could tell he was gone,
off in a new direction
heading out somewhere else and leaving all
or nothing behind in those damn yellow eyes
staring out at me, out into a darkening world
where four men shuffled and laughed,
went in for coffee.

Inside with the rest of the crazy people
sitting down for coffee,
making words do all the work, talking shop, talking
park in the jargon of the civil servant man,
we know what chairs to sit in
we listen to the whirl of tongues
and the talk goes wildlife and telex and
choppers   it goes numbers and man-years and
stats it goes nuts for
fifteen minutes

and behind the words sometimes we hear
the anger and sometimes we hear the pettiness
and then the hurt. And someone tries to tell me
what this park really needs
what this park is really like, but I know already
it's like a dead coyote pup
lying out in the back of a warden's truck
waiting for the plastic bag we're
going to stuff him in and then we're going to
shove him in the freezer along with
the lamb that got it from the logging truck
along with a half dozen favourite
birds wiped out by cars, specimens now
and we'll save you that way, fella,
we'll cut off your head and throw it
up on the roof and wait till the bugs
clean you up and someday your skull will be
passed around
hand to human hand
and not one of them will be
afraid of you   not one of them will let himself know
how the last gasp was also like a sigh
how it was the wrong way to die   in the back of
a warden's truck   looking at steel
watched by humans   handled and pitied and
down on your side in the muck
a pup   seven months out of the den.

Coffee's over   we turn from our chairs
notice the blue sky outside
the cold sweet air that comes from the breath
of the animals and we hurry to our places
the crazy people and me, we gotta get back to our
paper work.

apart from them

The Eyes of the Body Are
Not the Eyes of the Mind

for Laura

You want to be lifted up to
windows now, you want to see
the world from an adult's eye and my arms
fold and lift and hold and now I know
what they have been made for, why
they lead out from beside the heart.
And for a moment what you see
stills your perfect body: horses small as ants,
ravens drifting by like bits of night.
The incredible movements
on the other side of the window
make you stop as if I have shown you a
miracle, although one leaf dropping down
would fill you up
completely. O there are moments
when the world is a light in your eyes.
They are your mother's eyes,
they believe the world is sky blue.

After a while you discover
the buttons on my shirt. You let the rest go.
You give me a kiss
(it took three weeks before you learned to
make the noise), and then remember
mum always gets one too.
All your life
you will remember us, you will remember
the mountains of your birth, the books and bears,
the four colours of winter that always end with
snow white. You'll do all right and all we ever do is
point things out, show you what it's like
above the crowds, all we can ever do is
hold you, little spy face,
keep the world safe another dozen years.

The Development Blues

*

A big thing
they all said it was coming, a big one this time
as if it could be caught
like fish or disease
like money, change, or jobs

Businesses won't fail anymore
The Timber Inn Restaurant used to be
The Embers
               which burned down in hamburger fat,
which used to be a
second hand store
               tires tins antiques
Before that, a blonde took over
(from California or somewhere south) but she
was too soon
               Here before the money
Yeah there's a big thing coming
What are we going to do when it
gets here
               Catch it I guess
               There's five new restaurants to feed

(And before that it was
the Copper Cup, a hangout for kids who needed
someplace to go
               before they went Out ...)

*

It was the lake that
pulled them off the road, a chance for
beech, beer, sun, swimming
and soon we gave them shops
               the ski-hill made it
a year round place to be
               the rush was now

hammers swinging / everywhere / talk of deals
My house is suddenly
My Investment
Condominiums like forts around the lake
Boats thump the water
                              and in the shallows
plenty more weeds

(And late in the night
everyone's neighbour adds

Calgary oil dollars inside his head
pushing up the price
                              just a little more
then selling
skipping out in a day/   a new life

retiring to the Okanagan all night long)

*

Used to be
a farmer knew everyone in town and when he
went there

everyone knew him: god we were safe
the same people coming back every summer

five years ago
a stranger was worth the talk
if he stayed past Labour Day

now they're living here, building condos
pushing up ground and pipes and wire lines
Here

in the middle of
all the beautiful names:
clematis and late-blooming rabbitbrush, labrador tea

*

The young men love
their music, they play the local bars and sing
blue grass as if they were
happy / sad

or just plain aching from the labour:
trading time at the end of a stucco trowel,
swinging lumber up in the bare-back sun

the Lakeside Inn
fills with the people we used to call hippies, now turned
entrepreneurs, nobody misses out

the Inn was sold, then
sold again, more atmosphere
more people
finally we don't know who they are: strangers
who look like they're staying

And I can't blame them
I like it here myself and I love this music
tap it out and sing along
It's beer at the end of the day
in Fun Valley, B.C.
happy / sad and wise to the way

sewers   pour into the lake   naive contrast
          float by in the river

*

Five years ago
I finished my building and I'm living in it
day to day
when they tell me

It's Worth A Million

but you still can't eat the view
and there's more noise now although I can still
hear the bureaucrats
washing their hands and I wish I was

back then, listening to the music as the
whole-earthers play

off the road and deep in the bush
fires, sleepy children, dogs
back near cold creeks
stoned and dancing in the mountain firelight

in the green, by the poplars
in their young young light

The Truck that Committed Suicide

In one major operation he tore out her
big black heart of an engine and threw in another.
His fingers worked over her,
tightening and touching and leaving
little drops of blood that mixed with the oil and the mud.
He drove her on pavement and gravel and dirt,
on ice and muck and trails that ended like lines in the dust.
He drove her on the road to work,
down the Mile Hill where the deer
come out of the mountains on their way to the river for that is
their work, to get across the road, their daily task
looking both ways and taking their chances when the
big trucks come down on them, the loggers and the
cowboys, the tourists and the housewives up early,
the drunks trying hard in the middle of the night
with the booze inside them like a golden plastic fruit,
seeing a pair of golden eyes and sliding
into them, opening them up in the middle of the highway
that is a slab of noise and light, the wind
whips back and forth through their big mule ears, the hair
ruffles and they look like they're asleep,
can't quite get up yet. And later there is a stain
on the asphalt like old red paint where the ravens hop
forward and peer into the eyes as if to ask
one last question, and over near the edge there are
other birds taking their
share of the work as
his truck goes by.

Rolling down the hill into work
and the sight of ravens black as old women started
touching off nerves that went down deep, bringing back
a wave that went through the man and then
over him, a direct hit, leaning forward into something
not quite known and the truck felt it.
The two of them at once
crossed the yellow line, crossed the asphalt on the
other side and touched the guard rail.
There was a humping sound like the sigh of
extinction, a wrenching as the things that fit together
broke apart, doors swung open and she tipped and broke and
roared. His head
touched the windshield that broke then
shattered into all the smallest pieces,
some falling out and down to the ground
even before the two of them stopped at the bottom of
the Mile Hill, rolled up
against a tree with their black wheels spinning slowly, a tree
on fire now and burning with them and
adding its odd woody smell to their
oily exploding he / she smell, the smell
that would still cling and hold them together
after the necessary tasks of removal and identification,
after the separation and the final washing
there would still be that one vague and bodiless smell
it would stay the way it had formed in the last moment
out of paint and sweat and dust and blood,
one smell   so strong and rich and different it left other men sad
and gagging under nearby trees
retching and hawking and then recognizing once again
the sound of the ravens arriving for work
the smell in their hairless wings.

Behind a Counter of Oiled Wood

Behind a counter of oiled wood
before the change in town to new and new and more
Annie takes money from Old Mose,
Shuswap buying white bread
and his back bent but not (yet) his head

— behind all the exchanges
or before them or because or during
something went wrong, became new in town,
only the locals
get to hear the way it's told
as if there's more that can't be said (not now) —

whispers of a boy
taken out with a gang of boys, a girl in a new dress
and then someone lost, maybe pushed
in the high rock bush of Block 44
and Annie was there and says
nothing, she saw nothing

the search went three days
they found a toy
pink like a tongue under a juniper
no clothes some say
fast cars in town the night before
but no one talks and the sun goes quickly down
on each new rumour and Annie stands fast

now behind the white arborite
of the Food Barn at the end of town
and what she knows
is tied up and hung in her face
and when she doesn't take your money does she ever have (time)
to think:

the soil is thin here
nothing lies deep in this rock
— before the Indians started to die like Mose
   curled on the highway
   under the streaming new cars
   by digging down
   we all discovered bones —

hands on your bread she is (thinking):
bones, and the stinking past

Invermere

My friends live here,
caught in the frenzy of looking
and they are looking everywhere, they have
tried money and drugs and some of them have even tried
leaving. My friends,
some of us are lost because we want
what is good but we will not work for it any more,
we have been fooled before. Some of us
are ready to give up but then there are
the children among us,
and for a while we are happy
and even more confused.

My wife lives here, pulled back
from the edge of the world, crouched down deep
inside the dream of one family, one good friend.
She has a house and land,
she has bluebirds in her trees but she is
still afraid there is no real
chance, it has happened before,
late at night the telephone will ring
a voice will say
There has been an accident on the s-bend.
She will be thinking it has been easy
up till now, she will have to
pay her dues ...
                    but can't you remember
how you carried our kid through the town like a flag?
No, it is your daily work
to carry our deaths, your husband and your
child gone, flicked off by the world
where most of the people you know
you will know all your life and you will never say
more than hello.

My daughter is here.
Sometimes we walk to the river.
She rides my shoulders and she
grows up inside me. I am watching the world
in a different way now. I will
never be prepared for the worst it can do,
but I am watching, somehow I am even
getting it ready.

A young man goes for walks,
walks to the edge of the earth,
takes his kid and she shows him
stones so small they are almost
soil, she squats beside a flower.
He smiles when he sees the trails behind their house.
Someday she will find them, she will
climb to the top of the world then and it will
start over. She will climb out.

this is a precarious
domestic moment?
does he know why familial
feelings are vague even if strong?
does he have a political sense?
the poetry is vague and unmemorable.

Letters to an Ornithologist

for Kevin

1. *The Ornithologist Winters in Banff*

There are elk digging holes
in the winter outside your door and you think about
the dogs of Banff that come for a run in the morning.
The trans-Canada is out there, too,
the motels and the white arctic clouds of snow, the
skiers like tropical birds, in your room like a cave
with your sex and your books
while the stove clicks off and you imagine
the ornithologist re-united with his lover,
in your dreams the bittern pumps himself dry
and the heron spears the bright eyes of the frog.

Remember, in that cold mountain hold,
I came to visit. I lay down in the
stink of your stove at the foot of your bed.
I showed you poems, you gave me journals.
We had tea and then
the leaving, uneasy as first flight, and you
curled back inside that place where the
ravens fed on the red heart of the elk,
your life list postponed,
a world without wings, in a cage called Banff.

2. The Ornithologist Reaches Jasper

Somehow your letter gets through,
gets loaded and carried over three green passes.
The letter is hand-written, carefully,
each word as small as the climbers on Cavell:
these are the words of a field man up at three
walking his lines as the birds begin to sing.
So you like the mountains over there
and the girls have ski tans and Vibram soles.
Somehow this all comes through,
one note at a time, like the first bird of spring,
high and cold and unwashed in the perfect trees,
I can see you listening,
I can even imagine you
writing it all down.

So name a mountain after me sometime, it doesn't have to be
one of the big ones, doesn't even need to be
official although I can smell
administrative pull between the lines now that you have
landed a job in a national park and you can be one of those
hungry immigrants bent on saving
the Rockies. Hey, save one for me,
tilt one my way
because I can't get through anymore.
Mountains too high. Too many tourists.
Too many messages that get in the way.
So forget the naming of mountains, forget me.
Take a girl into the bushes, take a bird.
Tear it apart. Tear it apart, and
name its dying after me.

3. *The Ornithologist is Re-United with his Lover*

So here you are again on your featherbed of lust,
cautious as raptors,
pulling for veins and aimed like a shot – quick.
After all, who else could tell me
how birds fuck one another,
what they must feel
the moment all their sky turns fertile, becomes
egg. What will you do when
your nest is ready, when she flies
will her brightest feathers blow away?

But I have heard you laughing,
I have seen you giving each other room.
I know about that kind of
rubbing, you'd cross the continent
and come down in a single swoop just for a
touch, a peck, a preen.
And then I come and talk to you again,
filling in the spaces where the bodies never meet.
Once we talked of woman's love but later
you showed me the gun
and I smelled ducks dying over the lake,
coming down from the sky with a sob, with a jerk
that was the same as goodbye.

4. The Ornithologist Turns to Botany

You spent one summer, that was all it took,
sitting on an avalanche slope with a book.
You called it keying,
working with stamens, breathing in pollen,
alert for bears but did you hear the pine siskins further up,
they were weeping for attention while you held
blue bunch grass and the skinny stems of fescue.
A grey jay flirted in the trees,
a raven groaned and knew enough to fly away,
his beak stuck open in disgust.

Yes, you could tell me anything,
spilling Latin names like chaff through the talk.
On those clumsy slopes, I look away,
I kick up lumps of dirt.
You cross your legs and test the pull of the universe
on every stem. But the birds,
the birds are leaving early again this year.
So breathe the life of science into me, put the wind in me
that lifts the hawk to the sun and pulls
the sprout like a worm from the ground
as it ruffles your hair and ruffles mine,
as it gently turns the pages of that book.

5. The Ornithologist Moves Again

Everything is distance now
measured in the flight time between friends,
so much of the country must be crossed without thought,
in the dark, and I imagine you
on the other end of the line like a smile.
Your letter was happy
you mentioned wolves along the river
and I hear you quiver. When the birds sing,
think of spring, the country greening,
the time between us as small as a starling's eye.

When we meet in the mountains again
the curves of the earth will join at our feet.
Up there, in the sky that is
dark and blue, we will write our names someday
and then we will laugh
just to be together, pointing out
first birds coming down to us as if to announce
like the solid wall of the mountain that we have not
changed, we have only chosen
different ends of the river and after
all the talk we let the silence come in,
like the sound of rock and stone,
these places between the songs that give the song
its sound of the shared imperfect earth.

Out Walking

Sometimes I go out for walks
walks along the edge of the earth,
on goat paths along limestone sides of mountains, walks
on game trails that lead back into
the high tipped-up corners of valleys and I scare up
a wolverine running low to the ground like a devil badger
flinging back its head in the dark outline of
fang and tongue and fang. And I
stop at the edge of the creek
where the water is warm among the marks of things
that are webbed and hooved and clawed.

Sometimes I walk in the rain
when the great storms build.
They are born in all the inhuman places
and cannot be seen coming off their dark oceans.
The thunder breaks its back across our roofs
and the rain turns all its dark eyes on us.
A drop at a time, it wedges out
the holy artifacts, our fathers' graves
slide into the sea. The cool green
salad world surrounds us, makes its move to life
while we stand still, losing ground to the rain,
watching the mushrooms
that come thrusting up between us.
   Once I fell on my knees before it,
on my knees in the mud with the million tapping drops
sounding on my skull like all the drums
of Africa. I watched the clouds grind down the mountains.
I saw birds impale themselves like soldiers
on the high white lightning rods of men.
Everywhere the rain was sending me
a message: you are fed, you are
rain, your cities are dust,
you are here to witness the fertile places opening,
the dark warm places growing darker, deeper,
taking in the sound and the smell and the dumb life again.

Now the land slopes down into
mushrooms, moss, dark needles.
I go deep in a cave, smell the rain running through the land
but here the clay soil floats up through my hair and the light
goes down to the bottom, all the way back where it rests
on a white and weightless bone
and this I will carry home,
under my coat like a treasure, safe, dry.
There is a place above my fire for
the bones of the old lives when all the liquids have left
and the dust settles slowly
while I sit here and imagine blurred things on the mountain
grey shapes rising like pines
something wild running for the water, sinking down on its
knees at the river and turning to meet
wolves, dogs, or men.

Outside the rain slants down as if someone has thrown it,
it pulls the leaves to the sky like banners.
The clouds dissolve and set free the sun
where it rolls in a blue bonnet sky. And I think
the earth is the place to begin,

the ground around a door,
the meadow turning slowly into
forest: this is the first mystery
if only because it is not human and will not stop
the moment our own selves are rich enough
to do without
the earth around us: the great movements
of the soil will continue, the leaves
that turn the black and white of soil and sun
to green, the lake that is
rain that is lake again.
The tree flings off its seeds without compassion,
the wood gives up its sunshine in the flame
and none of us were asked
what part we want to play. Our place
is in the mind that sees the death of foxes,
birds, the weak and small
and goes beyond the pain, looks
beyond the mountain and into the mountain range.
We have the power that gives the bird
its name and raises us to
the gods that once we fashioned out of
bones. Out of the leaves and out of the earth
that made the bones, out of the earth
where all the bones will end.

relatively inconsequential / vague point
made in a pompous, long-winded way

repetitions of prepositions ?
Seems hollow

a poet talking to his poem ?

Wooding

We found the larches changing coats, turning gold,
we found them burning on their
high September hillsides ten miles from the town
that turned toward more sleep on its
Sunday morning bed, we were
past the clearing where the portable mill had stood and
left the hump of old sawdust full of
the only young lodgepole around, the truck
going slow, lugging and looking for
the perfect tree, one in
twenty acres while the nutcrackers bobbed in their flight
past the meadow where the elk had grazed and eaten
and already bedded down.

And we found it on the last skid trail
that went up through the trees like a rollercoaster ride,
we found it standing,
dead and clean and dry as a dollar bill.
So Gordon undercut and planned the pivot,
he looked to the top and he knew in his eye
which way it would go.
There were instructions, the last
uncertain laugh before the chainsaw came on, coughing
coughing, catching at last,
consuming us all while Gordon cut and looked
wedged it over centre
and dropped it down on the ground with a bounce.

Coming back from the fall, thirty rounds of
firewood stacked around the saw,
sometimes the clouds circled in like birds.
We talked about fuel bills and devastation,
we covered the future and
we dwelt like hungry dogs in the promises
we found. We noticed where we were at last
when we saw the lake and white banks of Windermere.
There was snow on Chisel again.
And we knew then something about coming down,
coming back into town where the people
stopped and watched our load of wood look easy going by:
we knew we had carried off a giant and this winter
our sleep would be warm with the forest.

loose, almost vapid, unconcentrated thinking
Inconsequential?
pompously gnomic

42

Walls

Sometimes these walls are wrong
but I am a young man and I do not mind
when they push me from room to room: here is
the room of the child, I can smell the crumbs;
here is where I sit and face the day;
here is the mirror where the faces are
checked and changed; here is food; here is love.

Like the walls of the heart, these walls
meet in the bitter little corners where the words of
last week's anger have fallen like a
pile of dust; these walls bleed;
they need to be cleaned, this one with its
smell of hands, another that is dry and dark
as a shadow. And I dream
all the rooms will be opened someday
a breeze like spring will carry off the past
we will live in a circle of sun.

But out in the streets
in the private scents that stroll by windows
there are rooms; even in the forest, at the ocean
we carry our delicate walls.

Sometimes now, I open a window,
I don't know where I am;
I travel white hallways and down into
the first room of the universe, the way it was
even before the first birth, the way it will be again.

But I am a young man and I do not mind
I keep one hand on the horizon
while the other has already learned to love
the closing of the door at the end of the day;
in the sheltering dark arms of the night
the walls fall quietly away.

Fear of Failure

Her first time on skis,
and the first real snow this winter,
she is unhappy with the spotlight, the snow, the very
air in her lungs: can't bend her knees
perfectly
right away – this is Five Years Old and I try to help
but the snow seems to be too much for us:
she whacks me on the knee
ski pole on cold bone
and I grab her and she cries
and I'm mad now cause I've done that wrong
and my record for being the kind of father I want to be
is still too few days.
And later I try to
explain but I must hold too tightly cause she
spins away and it's finished for her anyway, she
decides to take up skating while I
go over the words again: Look
Nobody's Good Right Away
At Anything
printing or putting on clothes or even
breathing: it's gotta be shaken out of you.
And I can't believe a man can stumble so much
with his child and just because she's alive
sure I believe in miracles
but what about when my blood goes numb
when the world rumbles and pains in the press
or the everyday lives make no headlines and die
choked on the pain all the way
or the endless complaints of money and sweat and
kids spitting at each other on the way to school
the taste of gas like death in the air.
I sit and listen to the future.

Do you know how it feels yet?
Do you sometimes feel it, little kid, little kid,
red coat against the snow, a
toboggan full of smiles, shake me
shake me loose, join me to the day:
I lack the drive
I slide down past the handholds of home
and I manage and scarcely care today
where the melting snow goes or takes me or ends.

Wilmer Sloughs, September

When I go to the Wilmer Sloughs
I look down on ducks, coots, the way
water spreads below and is calm in its bowl.
I walk the silty cliffs on the edge of their view,
I find a place where the wind has left a hollow
and I sit in a pocket of cotton stillness and I
hurt for the world.
Across the bowl and the river beyond the bowl,
across the valley, the mountains look up to their snow.
But here at my feet there is rubbish, I can see
a dump falling over a cliff, draining 300 feet into
brown water, there is smoke in the air and
above me, at the edge of an ocean of dust,
the pristine ozone dies.
And I have to think it over again,
how to live on the earth
and belong to the world of men.

I watch the cliffs curve down to the river.
One channel comes to meet them, willows
in her arms and the slough covers all the land
that cannot stand up and shake off water.
It dreams of an island covered in
one Douglas fir and the speckled nests of a hundred
long-necked geese. Every day it has felt
the folds of the muskrat hiding in her banks.
And I am surprised like the tadpole that
dances down the throat of the great blue heron.
A lump of clay falls from the cliff, lies wet
like animal dung. I can see the peaks over Wasa,
over the water where the goldeneye waits for
his eagle, I can see chlorophyll gift-wrapping mountains
in green, marching through the saddles that hang between the peaks,

waiting a million years for the nuthatch and the
squirrel, the grizzly
creeping out near the top, crossing the meadow like
a king. And down in the sloughs
I hear the hunters working late,
on the bridge over Toby
the fishermen cast their luck
while the station wagons pull to the edge of the road.
A slow mist is stepping out of the river.
The earth forgets to turn, trees
stand birdless in the wind. And I am
ready to leave now as the cliffs crumble again,
giving up a little prehistoric dust, the
glacial fluff and they send out their swallows, the little blue
ambassadors of earth while the magpie
flaps like a signal between the hills,
lands on an aspen that has turned on its amber lights
as if to let me know
I must hurry, the cold has come, there is not much time
to start again.

Death of a Warden

In the mountains, blue on blue and
full of blackflies, a young warden
is killed by his horse
kicked hard as iron on flesh — just once, and then the horse
spooks away

he is down
and slowly the world goes by
like his thoughts on their way ...

but the pain! and the goddam
horse and the eye-jumping
taste after taste coming up but
no sound in my mouth
these fingers gone straight stiff like this and blood
pumping, pumping
I can't ride this, I can't ride this
it's eating out my head, all this pain
like blue light inside my veins, I am busted
open like a thing stepped on in rain
I am puking myself up
it hooks me all the way out
it's passing and it's
passing

I've got to stand, look
up to the valley where the world begins and so
this is how it looks when it ends — that peak
caught in the sky, a curl of cloud, all earth
sloping to the river and I am
no longer young but like
the river as it goes past
as all things that are young and green
go past
The sun in the west, already?
It keeps piercing its way through,
winter into spring,

one, two, twenty-five years through and into
the season of the catkin
the time of the mating of the wild duck
when the sun returns to heat the stones and flow over
onto the green ground and the dusty boots
of wandering men
                    when peace come up through our feet
knowledge of the paths
leads us to the smell of a lake

but the pain and the damn
horse and all the careful how-to moves
failing me now
in clear sky day and everyone else has
the ordinary and I roll in the dirt
and why?
and why now lord is nothing like the ways
we die, horse and chrome and
murder and war and plutonium death ?
the wary wrong is here
under this spruce, looking out, and my blood
bubbles inside me like a call of crow
for even at the edge of the mountain
we are not safe: whatever it is that kills us
kills us here
Call it names but
ungraspable death is here to stay, call it
horse, it's just another word for the death that
makes the words break down and I can't find
the solid life in me
? *We are all crippled anyway*
information like cancer out of control, men and women leaving
men and women, children out of control
those whom we pledge our lives to
enter the work force
change
          limp into bed
and who we are raised to be
is no longer required and all the same
I am down

but still it is true
the tree has a similar complaint
the fish and the thrush, each green moment
dissolves into dust and I remember
we are born of the sun, we are
the earth and the sun mixed and the
sun stopped by the rock
and the rock that rose up in the clear air to think

if only I could be that quiet
would it be that hard to reach out here
open the door into death
see the power that
adds and subtracts from us all
I would not be afraid to touch it here
(this blood on my mouth
the smell of the dirt so near)
like these stones in the sun
I would stroke it on the cheek, I would guess
here is common ground

*

He turns into the fetal pain,
the home of blood and flies, the hole
as he waits for the other wardens
to pull in
the riderless horse, he is down and the jays come
dropping down beside him with a fluff
his poncho like a caul across the ground ...

o mum and dad and lord I know
this is a better place to die
I am open to the ancient breeze, here
on the guilt-free mountain,
the song of the thrush has reached deep inside
it has cut out the snake tongues of worry

and I am ready to receive
this thing slow-turning my way
the green bough bends down to meet me
here is my equal
catkin pollen is sugar in my eye

look the jays throw themselves
up to the air and I remember
to pray is to concentrate

my back against this tree, we are breathing together
my lungs full up to the edge with the pain
and then the air
is out in the world again, the tree takes it in and
I will not close my eyes
My hands are not hearing what I say
Mixture of earth and sun
place me
accept and prepare and this
spinning blood take as you would from any animal …

*

And the older wardens say
it could have happened to anyone and they tell
the story of Ed Carleton
kicked in the brisket and kicked in the head
and still red-faced today

they roll their smokes more thinly now
as they lean toward each other
but there is no version that doesn't end in death
and when it comes to one of their own this way
they go soft for a while
and they hide in their paperwork
or drive the grey highway all day …

October Moon

I.

The nights are colder now,
the blood of the animals thickens and like my own
takes up the hunt. Owls fly out of the moon;
elk wait for gutshot stickiness
down in the meadows where the bulls
thrash the saplings and the cows obey.

Moonlight covers these snow-dusty hills.
Tonight what is in me
matches the frost and decay in the air as the valley
fills with harvest smoke, as the
full moon swells and is large inside my sky.

2.

The door closes softly as a moth behind me
and I call to the moon, as if there might be
an answer, some sound never heard before on earth,
a butcher's noise among the planets,
but there is nothing

only my breathing, the vapour
going out of me like a white life of its own.
I hear other things, not the owl or even
the bats slicing through their bubble of air.
In the village below, a man looks up from his paper
hears dull movements in his
children's bedroom where the toys glow in the light.
Even the mice in their fields are still.

And then we hear it,
we hear it in the back of the skull, in the
heart we hear the laughter swelling, the terrible voice
starting up at first like the whisper of a child
then screaming out of our own mouths
a howl as the throat splits apart
and the hands come up like weapons.

3.

Tonight I will make a tall fire
and the flames will cut a circle in the sky.
For hours I will sit like this,
drugged on the flicker
while at the edge of the flames the animals
are padding through the colourless dark, on the hunt,

and then the daylight will come,
work will flow toward me and fill up my hands,
there will be reasons, light and shadow,
the clear outline of love on a face
the valley will hum

but sometimes my pulse will race,
it will be running through the memory of its night
and I will look up through the smoke and high above,
I will see the moon, pale as flesh:

these are the days when the night
does not go away and the nights are cold and long and
bright with death, these are the days of the moon.

End of Day

So often I have sat here,
my chair tipped back by the window, looking out
but not seeing the visible world, the
cars below going into the village
riding the Athalmer curve when the sun
breaks through, jumps into town
washes up and down and sweeps out to the sloughs,
the coyotes and the deer running on the levees
the muskrat hunched in disbelief.

But not seeing, so often
not bothering to locate specific places where the eye
might rest, settling instead
some short distance past the glass, just
hovering there like a hawk
or some small exotic bird that has lost
all sense of direction and is waiting for
the night, the collapse of light around its roost.

(There is one thing that breaks the
endless lines running out of the mountains:
a perfect tree, poplar-headed,
where the river is crossed, it stands among the
dark spruce and is round and maverick and
a thousand green flags in the last of the light.)

And then suddenly hammered by
doubt, I roll back through the hours and the working day
that is full of noise and bright flashes in
other peoples' eyes, beams running berserk behind
my own and I am caught in it like
something in fast water and the hurt
flows in my gut and enters ·
every part of me like lava in my veins and yet I have
fooled everyone today, they thought I was
properly attuned and ready to bear with them
the way things seem and are not.

(The river flows before me, a blue border.
The light is about to fail.
The tree is rigid. I have tried to
lock that moment in my eye.)

It is already dark by the edge of the water
where the stones glow for a moment
and then turn dark as the bottom of the lake.
Dark will step up the hill, up to the window.
Soon there will be a few scattered lights
and my own reflection in the glass, leaning back
pressed against the sweep of the light,
moving through the examination with my own judge now
as black as the night.

(And out in the night
the roots dig down for the river,
firm without thought, yet they too tremble in their journey
as if they know they can never
turn or look back while up above,
in the night breezes, the leaves seem to be so free.)

Touring B.C.

1.

The rivers and the mountains
send out their summertime invitations and we
go to them, again and again we close the cabin door,
climb to the top of the world.
Sometimes we cast out across the water, sometimes
we even forget
how much we had to be there.

2.

The rain has washed across its face
but the mountain has not changed, it has
cracked and ripped open clouds of snow,
it has seen the trees approaching
but nothing has changed. The glacier
still stands on guard, aimed at the valley,
pointing down like a nerve.

3.

There is a wind in the desert
that whips and dances in the dunes. It
sticks in the roots of sage and it blasts off
the heads of trees. Sometimes it falls in the river
and leaves all the work for the sun.
Sometimes it passes through in the night,
sniffing at the sandtops, blowing them into the
lap of the moon.

4.

Inside each drop of rain,
the rain forest blooms. The sky pours down,
the ground swells with devil's club.
Somewhere, over there, day and night,
the trees struggle with their mosses.
Through the trees I get a
glimpse of animals, a moment that has
burst through from another world and I think
I am lucky, I am rich, I am hardly here at all.

5.

Here it is warm and ripe
but there is winter on a mountain not far away
and the trees know what happens next: the earth
takes back its leaves, makes a cover of
crisp gold, stitches the lake with ice.
Now we remember how we stood in the doorway one morning,
the wind blew through the cabin with the
sticky smell of spruce and we
planned the last trip, talking,
not talking, then turned inside,
lit the first of the
white flames of winter.

Looking at it Now
Summer '58 — Winter '79

1.

Looking at it now, from behind
this barricade of years — that summer greens
the slough shimmers with ducks
I sit by the horse trough under the leaves
by the damp earth that attracts the snakes and my
fear of them: a day I was twelve
spent in waiting, watching out across the earth
following the fence line until it curved into a neighbour
the thin deep path of the animals
willows over my head like wands
Or later on the edge of the road, kicking stones
as all the earth poured in
like water through the culvert, along the ditch
the beaver dams were risks
wet feet on the other side where lilies bloomed
year after year and would not change

    (And I want to throw out my hands
    and make a stop to it, that turning of the heart
    when you know something has
    slipped by and then I touch and grab
    those close to me, daughter and wife and sometimes
    the life that drives them
    moves me, carries me along, I walk the child to school
    every rock on the road needs to be
    examined and I know that already
    she is building. Soon it will be summer.
    I will be repeated and then I will be gone.)

And I can only see pieces that never counted then:
the first grass of spring
the smell of the car as I went into the city
the sliding of the landscape
and the journey that would somehow take me
into the only place
where no one else could stand.

2.

Into the city
with the magic of crowds and the stores that stayed open
all through the night and all this time
I was crouched
afraid of not-getting, or getting
less than the dreams that I had —
until a woman came and talked to me
the sun of that summer like the smell of the
country on her skin, the simple language of
nakedness at night as if there was no past
and time was a knot we untied and threw away

And the geography changes too
we move into mountains and winter locks us in
someone comes to wish us
happy new year and I cannot believe it again
although I can see around me
all the things I have collected, I can feel
all the layers under my skin but still
I cannot remember when they arrived, if it was
in this place, or in the past
when days were long and green and thin

    (The half-breeds camped near the house that year
    a pile of muskrat bones when they left
    I shot crows
    I smoked
    I wondered about the tits of a girl called
    Eleanor and walking home from school
    I threw stones in every puddle I saw
    There were picnics in the fall before
    the winter when my sister came home with
    her friend, then Christmas wine and the jack rabbit
    feeding behind the barn where the animals
    lived and were bred and died
    The snowbank behind the corral was
    twice my size and when I stood on it
    I could see
    across the field, the stubble, the opening in the west
    where trains were moved by the rules of the world
    and tomorrow was the answer to every question I had)

3.

All is gone, the barn pulled down, the horses dead,
even the train is replaced; now what is not held in my head
is lost, it never was
strong or clear enough to strike its line
across my brain. I remember, I remember, I remember
rats in the barn
the drake on the hen
miles of walking half-lost through poplar and bush

so the boy is never dead and now the man
watches as the seasons spill together
as each day the sun continues to set
without meaning and these hours of adulthood
cannot compare and do not survive

yet I learn to be still, to come back into
their smiles and the
quick slipping of hands into hands that makes the landscape
fade and blur, wherever we are,
we laugh together, we hug, we hang on and if we are
swept along, we stay together
new like the summer, like earth itself, a dream of earth
where love skids and explodes through our day

Journey: Going In / Getting Out

Getting beyond th ragged perimeters and
ugly edges thrown up by the clutter in myself,
going inside and getting past the grit stacked like factories
in my blood, then creeping into fields,
I want to go step by step
in that direction, into the full bloom of earth

There I can open to a centre that is
choked by the staleness of daily bread,
I can run parallel to words, at last
like starting up a mountain: getting above the forest
and then past the warm rocky nest of the marmots,
becoming small beneath the sky,
rising up somehow
like wind, like the air inside the wind
where all energies combine
and re-combine and are eliminated –

and sometimes finding there
only dreams, brains, calypso battles in the Friday night,
lust like the swing of a baseball bat or the guts of
an army feasting outside the gate,
flesh-headed soldiers dancing in the night –
sometimes finding there one who is already
waiting, standing up like a bear,
shivering at its first sight of me,
its face like a bull's-eye of blood –

Whether there is peace or war or truce,
whether I find good or nothing good,
still the body remains,
legs that have learned years ago
how to carry the sickening heart, how to
drag it down to the curve in the river
or to the quickening edge of the crevasse.
Body, wise like an animal,
hunted and chased through the tangle,
driven at times to the ground
but breaking through into the open,
always carrying its rider back to the sun and the fire,
step by step, this stranger
pulls me back to the deep caves of rest,
then pulls me out by the navel
until I am plugged into the peaceful bright
shock of the outer world — it penetrates
like a shaft from an early sun,
white arrow glancing off a mountain and going
far beneath the edges of the skin.

stale/prolix

Highlight Review

Think of the times I have laughed,
or think of love; think of the perfect day, it has
just a little sadness. While it lasts
all of this is good: the rain driving into the rock,
the rock before it leaps into the sea;
this day, this earth
the sun like a hand on my head.

Put that moment in a zoo, bronze it,
give me something to shoot for again.
Let me gamble, let me have a reason
to sacrifice the things in me that are kings
and I don't want to hear
what you and the rest are all saying
please, we will all be saying it soon,
please to the days that are passing
let me shuffle through them again.

Sometimes at night when I calculate
how I have earned my sleep, sometimes
there is noise and I think of waves
stretching their necks, day and night
they are crashing.
It is 11:23, things are dying.
Hours and hours of starlight and sun
slip and go by, I think of waves again

the days on the river when the whole high movement
of the dirt curves out of the white bloom of winter
and into one day, here & now on the river
and once again I am connected with
reasons for
rivers, trees, water between them like blood

I have stepped on the meaning of a rock
I have flown in the eye of the bird
Think of my brain full of earth

Columbia

1.

The creeks find their way down, dropping
through the stones and the boulders split with frost, they come
dropping to the riverbottom thick with mud and rushes,
they come
all the way down from the cold point of mountains,
they find their way into the bellies of mink and elk and eagles.
Their source is everywhere above us, and their movement
is down past us, turning into the land of ooze, it becomes
the river then: *Columbia.*

The creeks find their way down, gathered up
in lakes that hang
on the edges of mountains, caught up by
the masterminds of beaver. They gather in lakes
they gather in colours and rainbows
they collect in the aerial river moving south from Spilly,
storms that split and ride out the separate ranges miles above
the fishermen and farmers. The rain falls in their streets
it dumps on their backs
it falls on all the local names, it falls on the children
running on The Westside Road like flags in the wind
it falls on the newborn calves of March lying in their fields
like little brown suitcases, it falls
in the river then: *Columbia.*

The creeks take their time, learn to laugh
on their way down, they
roll through Indian plains of grey and sage
they roll past the first houses and then they flood
for they have seen their river
and they have heard its name: *Columbia, Columbia,*
it is another name for oxbows and levees and force.
They have seen one man flush out his garbage
while another man swims and drinks and dreams,

they are in a hurry now
they have heard the rumble of the dams and the
click-click of the pencils of engineers.
They are gathered under the wing of the fish hawk.
They wash the feet of the tourist.
There is no turning back.

And there are plans in the world for them.
There are maps of them when the
government and the people
take one river
change its ancient direction and push it into
the Columbia which will swell and sweep away
its banks, its trees and osprey, the fish will change,
the roads, the bridges will be
rebuilt, towns will go under, in the name of
progress we will watch them
move their houses out. The clear water will be gone,
in the spring there will be high water everywhere
and then mudflats, trees grey to the neck.

And I want to know
where are the people? Where
are the lovers who need the quiet river, the dip
and tilt of canoes? Where are the fighters?
We are crowded on the roads
we are hamstrung in our subdivisions and in our
services and we cannot get out.
We are gathered in our humanness
and each of our places has a separate smell like a thing
that a dog can tell. We are locked into
the local conversation and we are cautious as the
river deer and although we are not so beautiful
we too live half our lives with our noses
down at the ground. Where are the dreamers and the
rebels? Where are the ones who will rage,
the ones who will rage for an end to this thing?

We are hiding again, we are waiting,
we want to be ready with all the force we have
just before the very end,
the moment someone decides we need
more power, more power and things, and we will
sell the river then. We will let it be flooded
and we will do it for our things,
for our duty to the plastic things
and we will not want it but we will not
know how to stop. We will be washed over by television,
by lawnmowers and trucks and bright lights,
we will stay plugged in.
It will take ten years but we will make it,
we will be the Okanagan once again,
hot plain of factories.
And I want to know why it is like this.

The mountains come down with their creeks,
come down into hills and humps and benches.
Ten thousand years ago the ice stood here
high as the wingless clouds and it rubbed and rounded
mountains, it re-shuffled earth and rock
into kames and kettles and plains. It left us
eskers, cracks that filled with
sand pouring into the ice and when the ice was gone
it left long hills with a bellyful of sand.
For ten thousand years more
the rain fell and took up roots inside
the rocks. And the local names
are here to show it: Sawtooth Range and Chisel Peak.
But that is a long way back.
That is back to the first naming of creeks,
Toby and Goldie and Dutch,
Horsethief and Ben Abel, that man with whiskers
and a huge horse and wildness in his eyes.
I want to know his name for the creek.
I want to stand that man on top of an esker,
and let him talk, and then I'll tell him
his creek is up for sale.

2.

On the river, when you are
finally on the river and you are alone with a friend,
you can finally
let it go, all the rancor and the displacement
it does not matter here. They say I am a newcomer
and I say to them
get down to the river and say that, watch
the ducks fly up in laughter. This friend
knows the songs of all the birds by heart,
they are part of his heart
they are the reason he has a fighter's heart, he
stands up in the boat to see above the levees
and through the great black trees that
stand guard along the bank. We speak of
trees and mink and let it go.

It goes by
and we drift through the world again like children,
after the first hour
we have settled in. An eagle hangs above us
like a man crucified to the sky.
There is a dead thing ahead, an elk
that crashed through the ice and turned instantly
to food for the ling, the suckered fish
following the canoe like shadows.
There is wind
there is the surface of the water rippled and stretched
by the wind. There is rot and the
smell of rot and there is finally a
blankness in the mind, it lets the eyes see again,
and the eyes look out from the dark heart itself
and they let in the timeless light of the wild.

They see the banks of the river,
carved and broken and sometimes dropping down
like mud, pale faceless mud. They see
line of sand upon line of gravel and we wonder out loud
how long it took,
we want to know about
the writing between the lines. But we do not expect
an answer, that is not why we are here today.
We want to feel   "sublime"
small because then we will also feel
as large as the eagle and the white world of swans.

We will defer
to the river and to all the universe.
We will allow ourselves to be captured.
We will stop on a gravel bar
the boat will groan against the stones.
We will part the leaves and look into the
? wet heart of the meadow, there will be
paths to follow, there will be
muscles to move and the delicate love songs of
chickadees. There will not be
other people, there will be no complicity. >? anti-social

3.

When I first came here
I did not know their names for the world, its
things. They said fish hawk and I said osprey.
When I first came here
I went alone to the tracks, down to the
CPR with its clang and then the hiss of sound
that is the hiss of power. I heard its horn
that has been here so long
it does not belong to us. I went alone
to meet the people. I looked in all the faces,
I saw women at their windows, standing with their
arms in the sink. I saw silent men
stepping out of their houses in the morning, they were
caught by something, caught by the neck and by
the bones. I wanted to take the train,
catch the boxcars strung out like beads in the sun,
follow out its sound as if it were
a song of my own, howling with relief to be going.
When I first came here
I came like the tourists:
I had the smell of the road on my hands,
I did not know I was home, yet this
grew out of me like mountains out of the ground, *?*
the mountains that disappear blue on blue
from my door as I piled up
the time, and found
enough friends and the secret places
only locals know.
I grew fond of all the faces,
I knew their stories and mistakes and still
they took me in, let me settle
and understood when I asked
where are the people, where are all   *naive leap*
the good people? now that here
at the end of the road there are plans
for the source of a valley, its movements, its
rhythms, its river.

4.

In the backwaters the muck
settles slowly and it gives birth there,
it gives a man a chance to see
where the story first began. We sink in the mud
and we see the tracks of a great blue heron
wide as a child's hand.

And we see the colourful gleam
of gasoline. We see surveyor's tape
tagged to the trees like ribbons.
We have been here before
and I want to know where it will end.

O blue valley
I came west as far as I could
and built a house that looks back, looks east and looks
into the river, the place where it
bulges and laps against the tracks.
It looks into the dark eye of the swan.
It places me. I am within the flow.
There is no turning back.

And this is where it will end,
in a moment of fury when we
stand with our children and we block the machines,
when we tear our page from the maps
and we drive the consultants
back to their shame. There will be no fear
we will go down to the water and into the dream, it will
flow through us
or it will sweep us away.

5.

Columbia, your water moves inside my blood.
You, too, are confined and you break out of it,
sometimes you reach as high as our windows
and you rattle the doorknobs of Athalmer.
They are going after you,
all the good people of the country, they are
going to make you better. They are going to make you
serve. And when I ask you
where are your friends
                          there is only silence.
It is the sound of mountains coming down
with their creeks, coming down through the ice.
It is the sound of men fighting, men
failing to fight, and men

passing. *Columbia,* you have that on your side.
Your water will wash our bones.
Your water will cleanse us.
Your water will take us all home.